For John Hill. Always a healthy suspicion of the establishment.

BY DAVID MODELL WORDS BY KEVIN TOOLIS

TORY STORY

VISION ON

WWW.VISIONONPUBLISHING.COM

POLITICAL PARTIES ARE TRIBES

Each has a distinct character. They have their own territory from which they launch attacks on their opponents but from which they seldom venture. Tribal loyalty is all. The precise nuances of tribal law do not greatly detain its members, but there is a tribal dialect, a language almost, which is virtually unintelligible to the outside world but which will have immense totemic significance for the tribe itself. This is not religion, but one could be forgiven for thinking that, to paraphrase the late Bill Shankley's immortal words, it's much more important than mere life or death. Indeed, tribes are immensely loyal to their departed gods and erect monuments to them, and pray at their shrines. Anyone who has witnessed Lady Thatcher's recent Conference performances can have no doubt about that. And, like all tribes, the political party is a family. You laugh and cry together. You feast together and fight the enemy shoulder to shoulder, but never as viciously as you fight yourselves. Yet however brutal the family squabbles, irrational, visceral, morbid hatred of the enemy will still emerge when the great Thousand Years' War enters its next bloody episode and the tribe dons its ritual colours and once more mans the barricades.

The party member – never to be confused with the sympathiser or even regular voter – is a special animal. It may be true that you have to be slightly mad to belong to any party, but having been a fully paid-up member for more than twenty years of Europe's oldest tribe, the British Conservative party, my own take is that you are simply innoculated with a virus you can never shake off. Once a political animal, always a political animal.

Political parties are also an extraordinary cocktail of volunteers and professionals. The members are technically in charge and so are impossible to control. They are true individualists. The great British eccentric is all too obviously alive and well on these pages. You can also distinguish the hired hands. They know they can never win. If the tribe wins, the volunteers will claim the credit. If they lose, it will be the poor pressed foot-soldiers who bear the brunt of tribal anger. Leaders too are judged harshly. Success in battle is all, and the leader is never secure unless, as seldom happens, the next victory is assured.

These wonderful pictures are their own story and their own powerful insight. Their subjects are sometimes recognisable but more often not. And it is here that the real unselfconscious, unvarnished character of the Tory tribe emerges, in dress, in style, in their groups, in quiet corners and in rowdy halls. When you have enjoyed this book you will know more about the Conservative party than any political scientist could impart in a tome ten times the weight. This is indeed the real party I have known for all of my adult life. It is occasionally as awful, as banal, as ludicrous and as eccentric as it looks. I hope the book conveys a little too of the fun, the camaraderie, the genuine friendship based on shared goals which I have felt over those years. And you should know too that, for all our occasional inability to see ourselves as others see us, this is still the party that I love and will never leave.

Steven Norris

POLITICS IS THE ASSUMPTION OF POWER

You pretend to the outside world that this disparate, warring amalgam of dreamers – the ambitious, the fixated, the prejudiced, the Conservative and Unionist Party of the United Kingdom – are 'the natural party of government', and the outside world takes you at your word.

You act as if you were leading the country, or are about to. It's a trick, a gimmick. Never walk, swagger. Occupy the stage, make it your own. Squeeze them out. Block their light. Choke them. Make them - irrelevant.

And then one day you are. In. Power.

Jobs are given out. Secretary of State of This, PPS of That, special advisors, researchers, the party delegate of Somehamptonshire, down, down to the earnest tea-stand volunteer. Offices are apportioned, policies declared, some differences are made.

Civil servants formulate policy, send you memos in red boxes, the trappings of State. You largely agree, and sign. You have

authority, calibrated, hemmed in by other departments, stiff Permanent Secretaries, and the other jostlers in the pack. But Authority. You were born for this, and more.
Power is temporal and provisional, but it is there. You look in the mirrors of the faces of civil servants, the press, the envious, and the poor fools of the party faithful. They look up, not down. They affirm that you belong here. They all want a piece of you, a touch of your clothes, a smile, a handshake, a little bit of majesty. Always look them in the eye. They are less, you are more. It's impossible not to believe in your own self-importance.

The Power lasted a long time: our glorious perpetual summer after that winter of discontent. 1979. It lasted so long it seemed it always should. Labour were a joke. Children grew up not knowing of an era before Margaret. B.T.: Before Thatcher.

Margaret, Margaret, Queen of Tory Hearts. She had to go in the end though.

In Office you are protected; insulated from the weather, and the world. The machine runs smooth. Memo, policy, tick, memo. It could all be make-believe but the wheel does turn. The People largely obey. No smoking in the Underground! Seat-belts are compulsory! Reform/smash the Unions! Yes! The poll tax! A misreading, true, but retrieved, in the end. Boom and bust. And boom.

Taxes were always going down even when they were going up. It's about balance, the economy, decent law-abiding families, the married, and pensioners who worked all their lives and saved hard for the future. The little man. Red tape and Government off their backs. And business too. Create the right conditions. Support the police. Tradition. Change nothing unless you have to. And instinct. The Conservative Way. You don't need to explain. It's there, obvious, a natural force. The way people should be.

We know who we are. And we know what we're against: Irish terrorists, taxes, crime, scroungers, the Labour party, world socialism wherever it exists, and (delicately with this one) too many foreigners. Europe too. A tricky one. We must preserve our Sovereignty. Somehow.

You're born with it, really. Once a Tory, always a Tory. Who remembers last year's Budget anyway?
The phone rings a lot and the things you said yesterday are reproduced in today's newspapers. The media are voracious: BBC PM, AM, Wales, Gaels, Radio Leeds, Radio Tweed, TV Mead; an audience of insomniacs, nerds, other politicos (but all carefully watched in Downing Street), and those eager for a blunder. You have to be careful, keep to the line, watch your back. The Today programme is a must. If you get on, good. Humphrys - Naughtie. Ignore them; speak to the audience. The handlers will always say it does mean something, the argument is being won, somewhere. And they're right. If you can convince yourself, then you'll convince others.

Napoleon said it's possible, at the start, to give an impetus to events but after that they drag you along. That's what happened. **A.M.: After Margaret.**

CHAPTER ONE
POWER FAILURE

1993. John Major had a destiny in 1990. Margaret had fallen. He was the historical necessity, the 'weak, transitional leader', a Kerensky waiting to be clobbered by Lenin, a little man who arrives at the right moment to make things worse and is then quickly overthrown. His epitaph, pre-scripted, said he should lose, but he won. 1992. He defied history. A great campaign. Fear, the double whammy. We had it right, or the ad-men did. We were Lucky. The People were afraid. Better the devil. And the Party went on. But things did not go well.

There are no revolutions in democratic politics. Parties splinter from within when the outward bonds break in the face of an unavoidable enemy: Europe, the euro. The desire to govern, the collective longing of the leadership to be in power at all costs, is contradicted by the aim of each faction and their leader to triumph. The power of the Leader wanes, the mirror darkens, the wheel amongst his own ministers, first, stops turning.

Power is always hidden, elusive, shifting. Division leaks. It affirms itself in the shadows, the whisper; in the determination of the hopeless to make a stand for principle, and election, and the circling calculation of rival kings. Better to be feared than loved. Better to be hated than laughed at. There is no recovery from derision. Just contest.

NEWS CAME FROM ANOTHER PROVINCE OF WAR, DIVISION, RESTLESSNESS...

MICHAEL BRUNSON ON COLLEGE GREEN REPORTING THE GOVERNMENT'S DEFEAT ON THE MAASTRICHT DEBATE; AUGUST 1993

THE AGED, TOO, HAD THEIR PART TO PLAY.
EDWARD HEATH GIVES A RADIO INTERVIEW ON COLLEGE GREEN DURING THE MAASTRICHT DEBATE; AUGUST 1993

A FEVER IN THE LAND AND THE PEOPLE HUNG ON EVERY WORD.
MEMBERS OF THE PUBLIC LISTEN TO GILLIAN SHEPHERD DURING A TV INTERVIEW
AT THE TIME OF THE LEADERSHIP ELECTION COLLEGE GREEN, JULY 1995

...AND THE HOPELESS DETERMINED TO STAND FOR PRINCIPLE, AND ELECTION.
JOHN REDWOOD IN THE BBC WESTMINSTER STUDIOS, PREPARING FOR AN INTERVIEW
DURING HIS BID FOR THE PARTY LEADERSHIP; JULY 1995

OTHERS JUST MADE A STAND.
BILL CASH, LEADER OF THE ANTI-MAJOR REBELS, WAITS TO BE INTERVIEWED
IN THE BBC STUDIOS DURING THE LEADERSHIP ELECTION; WESTMINSTER, JULY 1995

VANITY IS THE MIRROR IN WHICH WE SEE OURSELVES, AND OUR AMBITIONS, FALTER.
NORMAN LAMONT PREPARES TO APPEAR ON CAMERA; WESTMINSTER, JULY 1995

I LISTENED OUT FOR A SIGNAL. BUT NO ANSWER RETURNED.
A_AN CLARK WATCHES AN INTERVIEW; WESTMINSTER, JULY 1995

ON COLLEGE GREEN, AMIDST THE BABBLE OF A THOUSAND VOICES, WORD CAME.
MEMBERS OF THE PUBLIC LISTEN TO THE RESULTS OF THE LEADERSHIP ELECTION; JULY 1995

THE TELLERS OF FORTUNE.
PETER TEMPLE-MORRIS, IAN TAYLOR AND MICHAEL ANCRAM
JOT DOWN THE RESULTS OF THE LEADERSHIP ELECTION;
COLLEGE GREEN, JULY 1995

LEADER, AGAIN.
PREVIOUS: JOHN MAJOR MAKES
HIS ADDRESS TO THE PARTY
CONFERENCE; BLACKPOOL,
OCTOBER 1995

MICHAEL PORTILLO.
DEFENCE SECRETARY TALKS TO
JOURNALISTS IN THE IMPERIAL
HOTEL, THE EVENING AFTER
GIVING HIS SPEECH TO THE
PARTY CONFERENCE;
BLACKPOOL, OCTOBER 1995

WILLIAM HAGUE.
WELSH SECRETARY GIVES
AN INTERVIEW IN THE
IMPERIAL HOTEL;
BLACKPOOL, OCTOBER 1995

GOING HOME.
PETER LILLEY AT BLACKPOOL STATION AFTER THE
ANNUAL PARTY CONFERENCE; OCTOBER 1995

CHAPTER TWO
HOLDING ON

1996. The natural party of government slowly dismembers itself one radio interview, one TV appearance, one comment article at a time. One day there is no united line. The pace accelerates; the disintegration of the Party confirms the existence of the Party. We are still at the centre of the world! The newspapers are full of conspiracies. The stock for scandals is high – brown envelopes and that treacherous little Egyptian shopkeeper. The price for policies, low.

The Enemy is suddenly clever. Smith, the Scottish lawyer, dead on the bathroom floor. Replaced. Blair, smirking like a schoolboy. Youthful. But full of the Dark Arts. Fat Cats, fat cats, sleaze, on and on till the last syllable. Every face turned against us.

Soon the sound booms; the lenses, the notebooks are no longer there to record the rulers but to spectate at a public execution. The People, the Great Indifferent, the mass in the terraced houses that whiz by in a blur, the crowd out there beyond the realm of pollsters, pundits, parliament; have grown tired of this same old band of yapping idiots. Doom.

The Party is dying, it's only breathing on the life-support apparatus of Government: Downing Street, ministerial cars, the Prime Minister. Tokens. The petty thefts start from Government offices. Mementos are taken, remembrances; headed notepaper, pens, trinkets, future relics of the time we were in Government. The Exile begins before the Election.

SETTING THE STAGE.
PREVIOUS: ANDREW MACKAY AND ALISTAIR GOODLAD, GOVERNMENT CHIEF WHIPS,
AT THE EDGE OF THE PARTY CONFERENCE STAGE; BOURNEMOUTH, OCTOBER 1996

ALL EYES UPON THE LEADER.
JOHN MAJOR DURING HIS CONFERENCE SPEECH;
BOURNEMOUTH, OCTOBER 1996

OH, WE DO LOVE TO BE BESIDE THE TORY SEASIDE...
JOHN MAJOR GOES ON A WALKABOUT ALONG THE BOURNEMOUTH
SEAFRONT; OCTOBER 1996

TIME, AND THE PARTY, WAIT FOR NO MAN.
JOHN SELWYN-GUMMER, FORMER AGRICULTURE MINISTER, PREPARES TO WIND UP A DEBATE
AT THE ANNUAL PARTY CONFERENCE: BOURNEMOUTH, OCTOBER 1996

JERUSALEM, JERUSALEM, OH ENGLAND, MY JERUSALEM!
AT THE CONFERENCE BALL, MEMBERS OF THE PARTY LISTEN TO THE
COMEDIAN JIM DAVIDSON: BOURNEMOUTH, OCTOBER 1996

BEGOTTEN, NOT MADE.
DELEGATES APPLAUD A SPEECH; PARTY
CONFERENCE, BOURNEMOUTH, OCTOBER 1996

FROM A CORNER DARKLY GLEAMING.
PARTY WORKERS LISTEN TO A SPEECH AT THE EDGE OF THE
CONFERENCE HALL; BOURNEMOUTH, OCTOBER 1996

AN HOUR UPON THE STAGE.
PETER LILLEY GIVES A TV INTERVIEW AT THE END OF THE PARTY CONFERENCE
OUTS DE THE BOURNEMOUTH INTERNATIONAL CENTRE; OCTOBER 1996

WAITING FOR THE CHOSEN PEOPLE.
A PARTY MEMBER LISTENS TO A SPEECH DURING A FRINGE
MEETING AT THE SPRING CONFERENCE; BATH, MARCH 1997

PREVIOUS: MICHAEL PORTILLO CAMPAIGNING IN THE
WIRRAL SOUTH BY-ELECTION; FEBRUARY 1997

UNDONE, UNDONE... LITTLE BROWN ENVELOPES AND A TREACHEROUS SHOPKEEPER.
NEIL AND CHRISTINE HAMILTON IN THE HOME OF A CONSTITUENT DURING THE GENERAL ELECTION
CAMPAIGN; TATTON, APRIL 1997

JUST WAITING...
A VOLUNTEER PARTY
WORKER DURING A PRIME
MINISTERIAL VISIT TO HALIFAX;
GENERAL ELECTION CAMPAIGN,
APRIL 1997

SMILE, SMILE AND BE
A EUROPHILE VILLAIN.
CHANCELLOR OF THE
EXCHEQUER KENNETH CLARK
DURING A VISIT TO A
CONSERVATIVE CLUB IN
NORFOLK; GENERAL ELECTION
CAMPAIGN, APRIL 1997

ONCE A WARRIOR KING...
NEIL HAMILTON FLEES THE PURSUING PRESS PACK WHILE
CAMPAIGNING DURING THE GENERAL ELECTION; TATTON, APRIL 1997

THE WHISPER.
JOHN MAJOR AND PARTY CHAIRMAN BRIAN MAWHINNEY OUTSIDE CONSERVATIVE CENTRAL
OFFICE AT THE START OF THE GENERAL ELECTION CAMPAIGN; MARCH 1997

BOUNDLESS AND BARE, THE LONE AND LEVEL STANDS STRETCH FAR AWAY.
A PARTY WORKER AT THE SPRING CONFERENCE; BATH, MARCH 1997

GREETED BY VEHEMENT APATHY.
JOHN MAJOR TAKES ON HECKLERS DURING A CAMPAIGN STOP IN NORFOLK;
GENERAL ELECTION CAMPAIGN, APRIL 1997

LENSES AT A PUBLIC EXECUTION.
PREVIOUS: MARGARET THATCHER BECOMES THE SUBJECT OF INTENSE ATTENTION DURING A VISIT TO A
FOOTBALL GROUND IN MAIDSTONE; GENERAL ELECTION CAMPAIGN, APRIL 1997

'DIE, TORY, DIE.'
JOHN REDWOOD CANVASSING IN HIS CONSTITUENCY;
GENERAL ELECTION CAMPAIGN, APRIL 1997

AND THE BAND PLAYED ON...
TWO DAYS BEFORE THE 1997 GENERAL ELECTION, MICHAEL HESELTINE
WATCHES JOHN MAJOR THANK PARTY WORKERS AT
THE LAST RALLY OF THE CAMPAIGN; LONDON, APRIL 1997

UNTIL THE MUSIC RAN OUT.
PARTY MEMBERS AT THE LAST
RALLY BEFORE THE 1997
GENERAL ELECTION;
LONDON DOCKLANDS ARENA,
APRIL 1997

CHAPTER THREE
DEFEAT

1-2 May 1997. There is a final word, a final outcome for such things: Defeat. You see it best on Michael Portillo's face on the streets of London on that first post-election morning. The calculation has gone wrong; he has lost his seat and the pathway. He is tired, absent, staring into the middle-distance of nowhere. The camera catches the moment when the wheel finally stops. Dead. Hope is lost.

But the pretending must go on. Major went quickly. Hague replaced him. More of the same.

GENERAL
ELECTION

V IS FOR VICTORY AND D IS FOR...

PREVIOUS: CONSERVATIVE CENTRAL OFFICE, 2.00 AM ON THE NIGHT OF THE 1997 GENERAL ELECTION

THE LAST WATCH.
SENIOR PARTY MEMBERS WAIT OUTSIDE CONSERVATIVE CENTRAL OFFICE
FOR THE ARRIVAL OF JOHN MAJOR IN THE EARLY HOURS, 2 MAY 1997

THE ENDS OF DAYS...
DURING ELECTION NIGHT WILLIAM HAGUE GIVES A SERIES OF
MEDIA INTERVIEWS; CONSERVATIVE CENTRAL OFFICE, MAY 1997

IN THE MORNING BRIGHTLY DAWNING…
PARTY WORKERS SEEK COMFORT AFTER JOHN MAJOR'S DEPARTURE
FROM CONSERVATIVE CENTRAL OFFICE; 7.00 AM 2 MAY 1997

NOTHING SO BECAME HIS POWER THAN THE PARTING OF IT.
PREVIOUS: JOHN MAJOR LEAVES DOWNING STREET; 2 MAY 1997

EVEN HOPE IS LOST.
MICHAEL PORTILLO WALKS THE BACK STREETS OF WESTMINSTER IN SEARCH OF
HIS CAR AFTER LEAVING CONSERVATIVE CENTRAL OFFICE; 7.30 AM, 2 MAY 1997

CHAPTER FOUR
INTO THE WILDERNESS

1997. The illusion cannot afford contact with reality and on the public stage it never does. The worse of all things is somehow not. The loss of 171 MPs, over half the parliamentary party (it was a slaughter), is a just a marker, a regrouping point, on the road to further victory, says the new Leader. Troops must be led; battles must be fought. The war, although lost, continues.

72

STRANGERS IN A STRANGE LAND.

PREVIOUS: SEARCHING THE SEATING PLAN AT A FUND-RAISING DINNER IN THE GROUNDS OF A WEST MIDLANDS ESTATE; JUNE 1998

THE LORD OF FIELDS.
WILLIAM HAGUE WITH LOCAL COUNCIL MEMBERS ON THE
ROOF OF A NEW HOTEL; TEESIDE AIRPORT, JULY 1998

LEFT OR RIGHT?
WILLIAM HAGUE, PARTY LEADER, POSES FOR PHOTOGRAPHS WHILE
OPENING A NEW HOTEL; TEESIDE AIRPORT, JULY 1998

...AND STALE SANDWICHES FOR LUNCH.
HAGUE AND HIS TEAM PREPARE FOR PRIME MINISTER'S QUESTION TIME
IN HIS OFFICE AT CONSERVATIVE CENTRAL OFFICE; JULY 1998

FINDING THE LINE.
HAGUE AND LOCAL PRESS
OFFICER GRAHAM ROB IN THE
EXECUTIVE LOUNGE; TEESIDE
AIRPORT, JULY 1998

**HURRYING TO WAIT
BETWEEN ENGAGEMENTS.**
SEBASTIAN COE, WILLIAM
HAGUE'S CHIEF OF STAFF,
DURING A MEETING WITH WEST
COUNTRY FARMERS; JULY 1998

THE PEOPLE COLD, DISTRACTED, LISTLESS…
THE LEADER ADDRESSES PARTY MEMBERS AT A GOLF COURSE;
EAST MIDLANDS, JULY 1998

THE ECHO OF THE SELF-SAME WORDS IN EVERY HALL...

'WE ARE LISTENING.'
THE START OF A 'LISTENING TO BRITAIN' TOUR;
NORWICH TOWN HALL, JUNE 1998

DRESSED TO THE NINES... NINETEEN-FIFTIES.
LISTENING TO THE PARTY LEADER AT A FUND-RAISING DINNER; WEST MIDLANDS; JUNE 1998

STANDING FOR THE PARTY.
PLAYING AFTER-DINNER GAMES AT A FUND-RAISING EVENT; WEST MIDLANDS, JUNE 1998

EVERY FACE TURNED AGAINST US.
PREVIOUS: MEETING FARMERS AT THE EAST OF
ENGLAND SHOW; JUNE 1998

AMONGST THE FINAL FAITHFUL.
PARTY MEMBERS AT THE SWALEDALE AND
ARGARTHENDALE PIE AND PEA SUPPER;
NORTH YORKSHIRE, FEBRUARY 2001

CHAPTER FIVE
CLEAR BLUE WATER

1999. And in between, the revisiting of the same old ground; journeys amongst the dwindling greying faithful. Country towns, draughty hotels, the regional press, questions about farming. Blazers, floral prints, chiffon, the smell of hair-lacquer in the morning. The women are always dressed to the nines. But the clock stopped at the fifties — the nineteen-fifties. If you grabbed the Party by the neck all you'd feel is wrinkles. Natural wastage. Not the polls. That's what's killing us.

Oh yes, there are young. Keen, angry, and usually repetitious. A scattering of young men, misshapen and misbegotten, wearing their grandfathers' clothes and mouthing their fathers' words. Why do they come to us?

Empty spaces, chairs stacked, coffee and biscuits on the white tablecloth at the side. You hurry to wait between engagements. Raffles. Balls. Association Dinners. Stop at every table. Smile. Make them laugh. A joke about snooty Blair. They'll heave their guts out. Full sets of dentures on both sides. Always the same and always tight with the cash. Tories. £75 for the tombola; hardly pay for the petrol. Too crippled to knock on doors. Old, old, too old.

'We are listening.'
How many miles must a man travel to hear the echo of his own voice?

Meetings, meetings, meetings, a shadow Shadow Cabinet, an imitation of an imitation, intriguers, their eyes hungry.

Widdecombe, Portillo, the others; they look across, not up. Stale sandwiches for lunch.
I never liked a woman who preferred cats to children; unnatural. Portillo. A man to be watched. A man to be blocked. Danger.

Every day, another day. Tactics, the line, column inches conquered. It's like chess and football combined; one game across an acre of newsprint. It opens in the darkness of the early morning and goes on till the darkness of night, the score dissolving into the next game.

A revolving wardrobe of sound quotes: asylum, taxes, education, scandal, New Labour, must resign; our plans for guarantee, tax, allowance, promise, U-turn, change our minds. The wheels whirring without gripping. A toy car. No one is listening.

The Enemy fumbles, blunders, retreats, steals the ground. They argue amongst themselves. Captains fall. Mandelson: eyes like olives, black. He'd have done better on our side. Across the green floor of the House you best him time after time. But the victory is narrow. Blair is still smiling. Invincible. Fate. Private polls, public polls, each as bad as the other. Lost, losing, gone, before a ballot is cast.

They, the People, don't like you, William. Doubt if they ever will.

And the only answer you hear, or don't hear, inside your own head: 'Pretend, go on, never give in, because if you never give in then maybe you might win.'

AND FIGHT THEM TOO ON THE BEACHES.
JOHN SELWYN-GUMMER AT THE ANNUAL PARTY CONFERENCE;
BOURNEMOUTH, OCTOBER 2000

AS WEARY AS A HOLLOW MOON.
APPLAUDING WILLIAM HAGUE AT THE EASTWOOD
CONSTITUENCY DINNER; GLASGOW, JUNE 2000

WE ARE SHOUTING.
AN ANTI-HUNT PROTESTER SHOUTS AT PARTY CONFERENCE
DELEGATES DURING A COUNTRYSIDE RALLY; OCTOBER 2000

IN THE CORRIDORS OF CORRIDORS.
MEMBERS OF THE FRONT BENCH TEAM IN DISCUSSION
AFTER THE WEEKLY SHADOW CABINET MEETING;
WESTMINSTER, FEBRUARY 2001

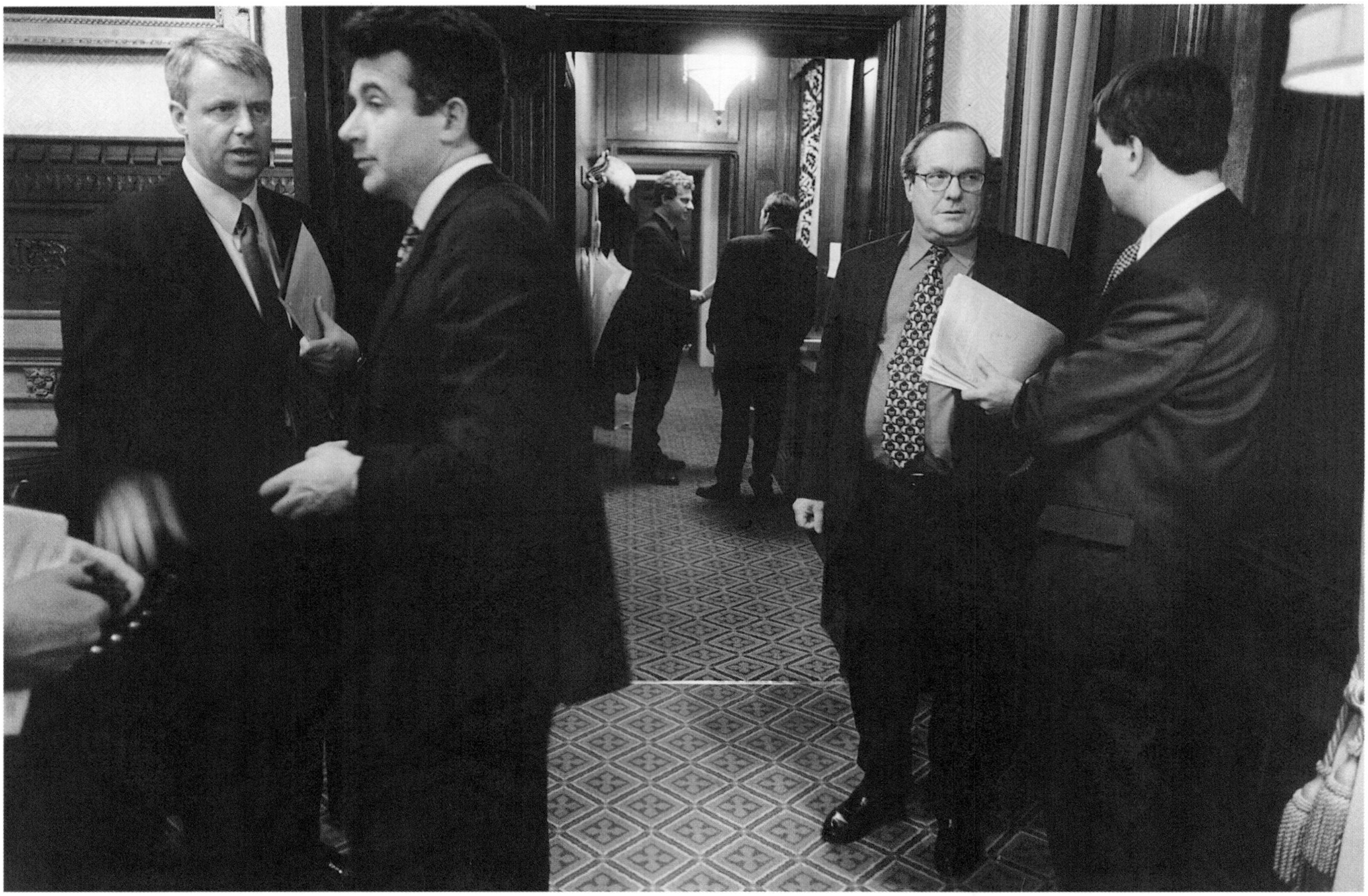

THE AYES ACROSS THE TABLE.
SHADOW CABINET MEETING; WESTMINSTER, FEBRUARY 2001

THE WINTER BALL 2000:
NO U-TURNS ARE FORBIDDEN.
PREVIOUS: LONDON, FEBRUARY 2001

THE PRIZEGIVING.
AWARDS ARE HANDED OUT TO
CONSERVATIVE ASSOCIATIONS FOR
FUND-RAISING ACTIVITIES; PARTY
CONFERENCE, OCTOBER 2000

PHEW! RED, WHITE AND BLUE.
RALLY FOR THE UNION;
BOURNEMOUTH, OCTOBER 2000

SQUARING THE PERFECT CIRCLE...

AND HERE I STAND.
SPEECH TO THE PARTY CONFERENCE; BOURNEMOUTH, OCTOBER 2000

LET THEM DRINK SOUP!
PARTY WORKERS AT A 'CHEESE
AND WINE' FUND-RAISING
EVENT IN A COUNCILLOR'S
HOME; THANET WEST,
JANUARY 2001

A SCATTERING OF YOUNG...

...MOUTHING THEIR FATHERS' WORDS.
LISTENING TO WILLIAM HAGUE AT THE EASTWOOD CONSTITUENCY DINNER; GLASGOW, JUNE 2000

AMONGST BELIEVERS...
PLAYING GAMES AT A FUND-RAISING DINNER; GLASGOW, JUNE 2000

...THE FAITH AND HANDBAGS TIGHTLY HELD.

MEMBERS OF THE CONSERVATIVE EUROPEAN UNION OF WOMEN AT A FUND-RAISING EVENT;
CHESHIRE, FEBRUARY 2001

A CHARACTER IN SEARCH OF A SET.
MICHAEL HESELTINE AT THE HIGH CLIFF HOTEL; BOURNEMOUTH, OCTOBER 2000

DO YOU RECOGNISE HIM FROM THE TELLY?
MICHAEL PORTILLO ON THE STREETS OF KENSINGTON AND CHELSEA DURING THE BY-ELECTION CAMPAIGN
WHICH RESULTED IN HIS RETURN TO WESTMINSTER; NOVEMBER 1999

MUGGED IN WESTMINSTER.
PREVIOUS: CAMPAIGNING WITH MICHAEL ANCRAM;
KENSINGTON AND CHELSEA, NOVEMBER 1999

THE RECKONING.
PARTY WORKERS WITH LISTS OF SUPPORTERS IN ASSOCIATION HEADQUARTERS ON THE NIGHT OF
THE BY-ELECTION; KENSINGTON AND CHELSEA, NOVEMBER 1999

AND THE RETURN.
INSPECTING CANVAS RETURNS IN ASSOCIATION HEADQUARTERS; NOVEMBER 1999

A COFFEE, AND THE SMELL OF SWEET VICTORY.
A BREAK ON THE CAMPAIGN TRAIL; NOVEMBER 1999

THE PEOPLE'S REPRESENTATIVES.
ELECTION NIGHT IN KENSINGTON AND CHELSEA TOWN HALL. MICHAEL PORTILLO PREPARES FOR THE
ANNOUNCEMENT OF HIS VICTORY; NOVEMBER 1999

BACK!

CHAPTER SIX

LOST LEADERS

2000. Party Conference is always bright, always upbeat; the audience drilled to clap even in the face of disaster. A throng of friends (including your enemies). A circus, really. It is a perfect circle, a perfect place. You speak, they clap. Clap, Speak, Clap, Speak. They know, they are waiting. Easy to please. Convinced before you say a word. The wheel spins. If somehow we could just bottle up the atmosphere, take it away with us, show the outside world. This is Right, this is the Way Forward, the Commonsense Revolution. They'd see what we mean.

On the last day of Conference, waiting for the Leader's Speech, the crowd is always especially excited. Their bags are packed, the first afternoon trains out booked, every seat taken. Oh, we do love to be beside the Tory seaside. But they are champing at the bit to get home for the weekend. It's almost a race. A few break away early and listen to the Speech in the car on the A31.

That never used to happen with Margaret. They always stayed right to the end because it mattered. It meant something. We were the natural party of Government.

We are, we were and will be again. We'll find a Leader who'll lead us back. The People will tire of Blair, New Labour - tinkering Tories. They'll want the real thing. One day they'll want us back. And we'll be there waiting for them, waiting in the wilderness.

I SEE THE PROMISED LAND.

PREVIOUS: APPLAUSE FOR THE PARTY LEADER AS HE ENTERS THE PLATFORM; BOURNEMOUTH PARTY CONFERENCE, OCTOBER 2000

OATHS AND OFFICES.
ANN WIDDECOMBE MEETS CONSERVATIVE ASSOCIATION
PARTY MEMBERS IN LEAMINGTON; JANUARY 2001

INTO THE BREACH FOR THE CONSERVATIVES AND THE CAT PROTECTION LEAGUE!
PHOTOCALL; LONDON, JANUARY 2001

MEETING THREE MEDIA MEN AND A MEMBER OF THE PUBLIC.
LEAMINGTON, JANUARY 2001

SHARING THE SEAT OF POWER.
PREVIOUS: PRE-ELECTION STRATEGY MEETING IN THE LEADER'S OFFICE;
CONSERVATIVE CENTRAL OFFICE, FEBRUARY 2001

THE WHISPER OF POWER DENIED.
PREPARING FOR A RADIO INTERVIEW, THE LEADER'S
TEAM WAITS IN THE NEXT ROOM; BRIGHTON, JUNE 2000

ANOTHER LONG DAY CLOSING.
PRE-SPEECH BRIEFING AT CONSERVATIVE
CENTRAL OFFICE; JANUARY 2001

PEDESTRIANS AT AN EXHIBITION.
PUBLICISING RURAL POLICING POLICY OUTSIDE A
CLOSED POLICE STATION; WEST MIDLANDS; JANUARY 2001

THE WAY FORWARD?
AT THE END OF THE WEEKLY OPPOSITION HOME AFFAIRS
TEAM MEETING; LONDON, JANUARY 2001

AMONGST THE ANORAKS…
A RALLY ON 'KEEP THE POUND DAY'; NORTH YORKSHIRE, FEBRUARY 2001

AND THE TELEVISION SETS.
A RECEPTION FOLLOWING AN APPEARANCE ON
THE 'DIMBELBY' SHOW; JANUARY 2001

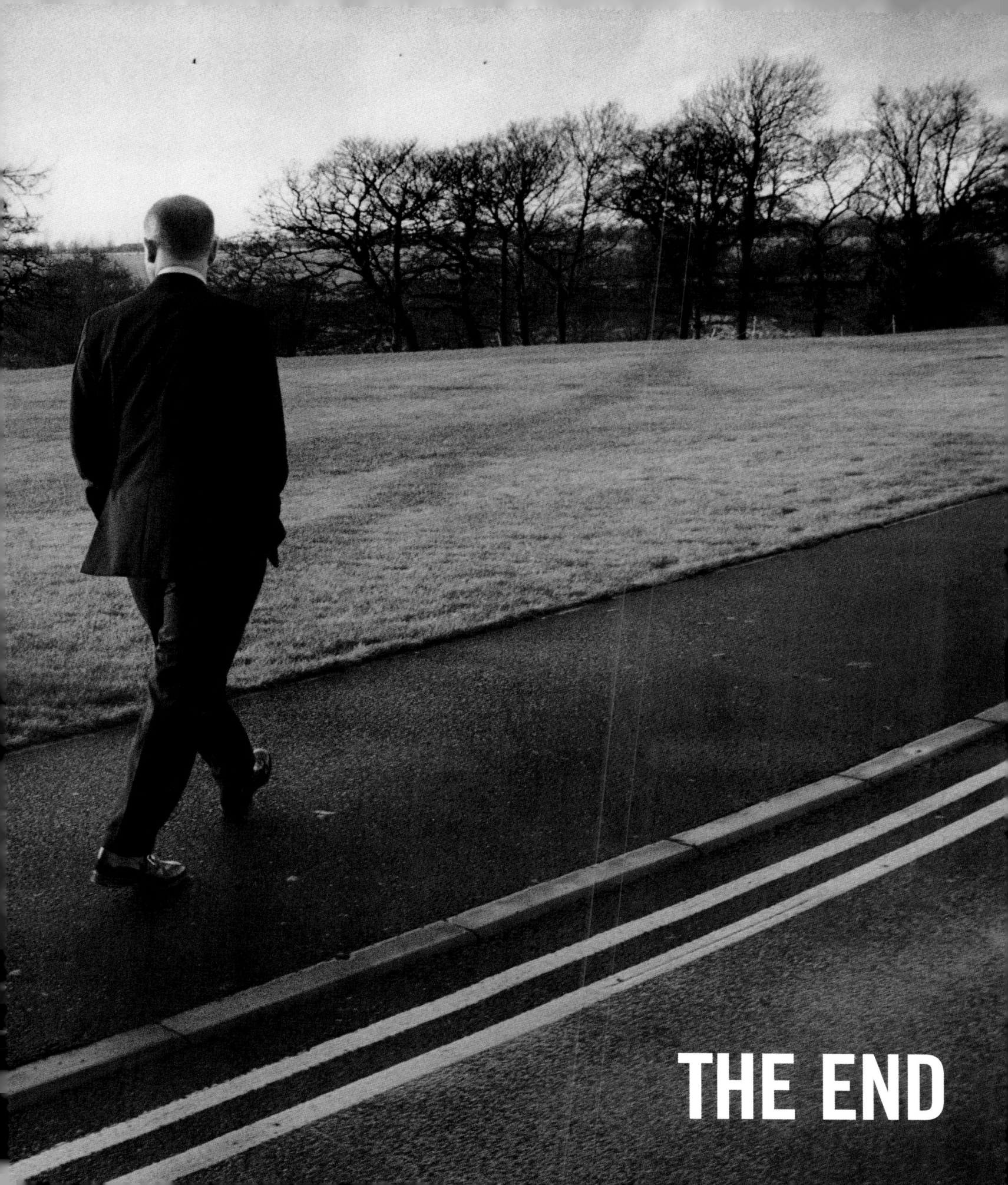

THE END

VISION ON THANKS:

Dan, Diana. Briar. Ronny and Ed at Vision On; Alan, Nina and Suzanne at Proud Galleries; Hector and all at Idea Generation; Tom and James at Argent, Kevin Toolis and Steven Norris.

DAVID MODELL THANKS:

firstly Colin Jacobson, who in various ways has made the major contribution to this project; the Picture Editors who have supported me along the way, especially Caroline Metcalfe. Nick Hall and Aiden Sullivan; my colleagues and the staff at IPG who have inspired me by their appreciation of the images (Tara and Seamus who found two of the best pictures in the book); Glen Brent for the excellent prints. Vision On for understanding it and for making the book happen; and to Madeleine- for the obvious reasons. Finally to the UK Conservative and Unionist Party for accepting me in an unexpected and open way.

Photography David Modell

Book design Saint Design

Foreword Steven Norris

Prologue and book text Kevin Toolis

Creative Director Kirk Teasdale

Managing Editor Zoe Manzi

Project Manager Sarah Marusek

Production Steve Savigear and Emily Moore

Reprographics Argent Colour

Print Grafiche Milani

Tory Story first published in Great Britain in 2001 by Vision On Publishing Ltd

112-116 Old Street

London EC1V 9BG

T +44 207 336 0766

F +44 207 336 0966

www.visiononpublishing.com

info@visiononpublishing.com

www.saintdesign.co.uk

mailbox@saintly.co.uk

ISBN 1903399254